DISNEP

ZOOTOPIA

THE ESSENTIAL GUIDE

WRITTEN BY VICTORIA SAXON

CONTENTS

INTRODUCTION

Scurry into Zootopia, a city of animals where prey and predators live side by side. It's a place that holds big dreams for all its dwellers, no matter their size, shape, or paw type.

When a missing mammal investigation blows wide open, new bunny cop on the block Judy must go on an adventure to solve Zootopia's biggest mystery. With some help from a street-smart fox, will Judy have the courage to crack a case that will shake up the whole city?

JUDY HOPPS

Judy Hopps may be a little bunny but she has a big ambition: to be the first rabbit cop in the city of Zootopia! Determined Judy is thrilled when she gets the chance to investigate a case—as this optimistic bunny says, Zootopia is the place "where anyone can be anything!"

Extra-long ears for great hearing

Bright eyes glint with enthusiasm.

Cream of the crop

Judy graduates from the Zootopia Police Academy at the top of her class. The cadet course includes sandstorms, boxing matches, and walls of ice—but Judy succeeds with courage and lots of hard work.

Rising star

Judy has been preparing her whole life to wear a police officer uniform. At the age of just 10, she wrote and starred in her own play about joining the police for the annual Carrot Days Talent Show!

Agile feet are good for hopping and running.

FACT FILE

⭐ **LIVES:** Downtown Zootopia

⭐ **HOBBIES:** Helping others, dreaming of making a difference

⭐ **LIKES:** Carrots, being prepared, hugs

Detective skills

Judy uses her sharp skills of observation as she searches for clues. Inside a limo, she finds polar bear fur, claw marks, the victim's wallet, and cocktail glasses etched with the letter "B." Interesting...

Run rabbit run

Officer Hopps is ready for action! Judy is not as strong as the other officers, but she's quick and nimble. She's also the only cop who is small enough to chase a thief through the tiny entrance into Little Rodentia (the rodent district).

Tough but soft

Friendly Judy is able to win over the crime boss, Mr. Big, after a misunderstanding. This kindhearted cop knows how to get along with others.

TOP 3...
REASONS TO BE A COP

1. To fight for justice!

2. To serve the citizens!

3. To make the world a better place!

STU AND BONNIE HOPPS

Stu and Bonnie have lived in Bunnyburrow their entire lives. They are proud of their farm and work hard to sell the crops. The Hopps like having all their family nearby, so they plan to keep in touch via regular videocalls with their daughter, Judy, now that she's moving to the city.

FACT FILE
Stu and Bonnie

★ **OCCUPATION:** Farmers, owners of Hopps Family Farms Produce

★ **HOBBIES:** Board games with the kids

★ **DISLIKES:** Wilted carrots, busy cities

Home, sweet home

Bonnie and Stu's farmhouse has had lots of room extensions added, to make sure all 276 of their sons and daughters have their own beds. It can get a bit squished!

Old fears

Stu worries a lot about almost everything— especially predators. He knows that, long ago, animals like bears, lions, and wolves were savage and dangerous. In his mind, a bunny can never be too careful. Stu never tires of telling Judy this!

Proud father

Emotional Stu cries often, whether he's happy or sad. No one is prouder of "Jude the Dude" (his pet name for Judy) when she graduates from the Zootopia Police Academy. And no one is more delighted when he finds out on a videocall that Judy is on parking duty— and out of harm's way.

> **"She's not a real cop! Our prayers have been answered!"** Stu
>
> **"Oh glorious day!"** Bonnie

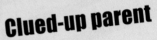

○●○○○ PB&J 🛜 8:40 PM

Velvety soft ears are pink inside.

Baseball cap shades face from hot sun.

Clued-up parent

Gentle mom Bonnie cares about all of her children, and can always tell if they feel bad by the way their ears droop. Bonnie is more sensible than Stu and a bit more excited to see Judy start her new life.

Mint green tank top

DID YOU KNOW?

Stu regularly plays cribbage (a card game) with a weasel!

Practical coveralls for driving tractor in muddy fields

Judy's paw holds smartphone.

THE BIG MOVE

Judy is one happy bunny—she's on her way to a new career in the city! As always, Judy wants to be prepared, so she has made lots of lists of things to remember to take. That way, she can focus on being the best officer in the ZPD.

CARRO[T] SNACKS SLICED, CHOPPED, WHOLE, JUICED!

CHECKBOOK!

Subway map!

Apartment address!

LUCKY CARROT PEN!

All aboard

Judy must go to Bunnyburrow Station to catch the Downtown Express. These fast trains zoom regularly to Zootopia Central Station, in the heart of the city.

Bye-bye, Bunnyburrow

Judy will miss her big family, especially as the city is many miles away. Her parents have already booked her a ticket back to visit!

Family photos!

Smartphone!

Light packing

Judy tries to travel light, so she can navigate the city streets and reach her new apartment easily. However, she does bring her favorite stuffed bunny toys with her.

Better safe than sorry

Judy knows foxes are perfectly safe these days, but she takes a pink bottle of fox repellent when Stu insists, to avoid a row. It's part of the "care package" he tries to give her—containing fox deterrent and a sizzling fox taser!

Flashlight!

Diploma!

Restaurant guide!

FOX REPELLENT!

Streetwise Zootopia guide book!

TRAIN TICKET!

Organized bunny

Before leaving home, Judy found and paid one month's rent on an apartment. She also studied Zootopia guides on everything from getting about town, to buying groceries for bunnies.

WELCOME TO ZOOTOPIA

Zootopia is a modern metropolis where all mammals—whether clawed or nailed, furry or fuzzy—can find the perfect habitat for any lifestyle. Visitors who are looking for fun can travel from the freezing tundra to the hottest deserts, in less than an hour!

Flowing waterfall

1

① Rainforest district

Rain-loving mammals such as jaguars enjoy the muggy Rainforest District. This wet habitat offers damp tree houses and lots of slippery roadways.

Looping train line

Bunnyburrow

② Downtown Zootopia

Whether old or new, huge or tiny, there are all sorts of different shops, offices, and mammal residences here. Zootopia Central Station is the main station in Downtown.

Snow-capped mountains of Tundratown

3 Little Rodentia

Little Rodentia is a perfectly tiny setting in Downtown for the city's smallest residents. It offers excellent restaurants and hotels, but only rodents can fit inside.

Desert palm tree

STRANGE BUT TRUE

Thousands of years ago, Zootopia was just a mammal watering hole, which grew slowly into a city. Today, it holds true to its claim of being a central gathering place.

4 Sahara Square

Ritzy Sahara Square is hot and dry. If mammals want to catch a bit of sun (or simply want to sweat out some water weight), this is the best district to visit!

MAYOR LIONHEART

Leodore Lionheart is the mayor of Zootopia. This large, loud, and slightly scary lion wants his city to shine. After all, this is the place where anyone can be anything, and Lionheart will do whatever it takes to keep city life running smoothly.

CRACK THE CASE

Lionheart's cover-up of the savage animals at Cliffside Asylum gives Judy an important insight—the mammals going savage are all predators!

POLICE

Graduation speech

Mayor Lionheart gives the speech at Judy's graduation. He's proud to see the first bunny cop graduate from the Zootopia Police Academy. (And he's also hoping it will help him win more votes.)

Forward thinker

Lionheart announces that Judy is the first graduate produced by his new scheme: the Mammal Inclusion Initiative. The scheme helps little animals get jobs usually held by larger animals.

Strange appearance

Judy and her sidekick, Nick, are shocked to spot Lionheart at a creepy asylum, during an investigation. As the mayor talks in secret, Judy records him on her smartphone. This politician is up to something fishy!

Bushy mane grabs attention.

FACT FILE

⭐ **LIKES:** Voters, a happy atmosphere in the city

⭐ **PERSONALITY:** Flashy, booming, charismatic

⭐ **DISLIKES:** Dealing with tricky problems in public, losing elections

Bold red tie held in place with clip.

Politician's smart, tailored suit

Claws always withdrawn in public.

Meek assistant

Assistant Mayor Bellwether is so meek and mild-mannered that the mayor finds her a bit irritating sometimes. She is always hovering near Lionheart's paws, or stumbling over his tail.

Big presence

Lionheart has a big voice, a big personality, and a big business suit. He wants to encourage Judy and anyone else to follow their dreams in Zootopia. He can also be a little gruff. Just ask Assistant Mayor Bellwether!

15

DOWNTOWN

Downtown Zootopia is a melting pot of claws, fur, and hooves. It is the place where the largest polar bears mingle with the littlest shrews. Newcomers can easily lose their way in the crowds—so watch your step to avoid crushing someone, or getting crushed!

TRUE OR FALSE?

Zootopia's population is made up of 90 percent prey animals.

Answer: True!

Animals on tour

Touring herds mingle in the city alongside office workers from City Hall and other buildings. Mammals who wish to travel in big herds, like buffalo, are urged to stick to the sidewalks and obey all traffic lights.

Nightlife

Downtown Zootopia is always buzzing, no matter how late it gets. Bright lights and cool music fill the night air. This is a city that never sleeps!

All sizes welcome

Every type of mammal is able to roam the city with ease. The walkways are built to withstand all sorts of weights and heights.

New apartment

Judy's home is small and shabby, but she loves it just the same. The desk acts as a table for microwave carrot dinners, and her bed may not be comfy, but her pile of bunny plushes fits on it just fine!

Gateway to the city

Judy's first stop in Zootopia is the busy train station. This huge building has lots of platforms and colorful billboards, as well as juice bars and cafés. It's a real sight for new arrivals!

Muscly cops enjoy testing their strength.

Blackboard with chalk diagram

Police chief's speaking podium

ZPD

The Zootopia Police Department (ZPD) boasts the toughest, smartest, and strongest mammals in the entire city. It's their job to keep the streets of Zootopia safe. The station is always loud, always busy, and there's always work to be done!

Tension on the team

Rhinoceros officer McHorn and his colleagues don't feel very friendly toward the new recruit—there's no way she's cut out to be a real cop! Judy's friendly fist bump backfires when he nearly knocks her over!

Huge headquarters

The ZPD building is a local landmark, with its grand front and grass-covered roof. There's plenty of space inside for all the thieves and thugs who are dragged in through the doors!

Map shows where missing mammals were last seen.

TOP 3...
THINGS THAT ANNOY CHIEF BOGO

1. The mayor interfering in police matters.

2. Bunny cops with delusions of grandeur.

3. Donut crumbs on case files.

The bullpen

At the start of each shift, the chief meets with his officers to update them on ongoing cases and distribute tasks. The team gathers in the bustling bullpen—a big room equipped with suitably huge desks and chairs.

19

BOGO AND CLAWHAUSER

Chief Bogo is gruff, grumpy, and grizzled. The Cape buffalo demands the best from his police officers. While Bogo is big and intimidating, ZPD's receptionist, Clawhauser, is just big. He's also a lot more cheerful!

Soft and fuzzy fur matches personality.

First come, first served

Clawhauser asks upset mammals to be patient and wait in line. He also tries to stop them from barging into Bogo's office without an appointment!

Hectic schedule

Clawhauser loves his job on the front desk, despite having to deal with visitors, organize case files, and help new recruits. He's also very passionate about snacks—especially donuts!

Cereal crumbs scattered down his front.

Tight-fitting shirt due to love of donuts

FACT FILE

⭐ **SPECIES:** Cheetah

⭐ **NOTABLE FEATURES:** Spotty orange and black fur, chubby cheeks

⭐ **LIKES:** Having a whole box of treats to himself.

20

No nonsense

As the Chief of Police, Bogo runs a tight bullpen at the ZPD. Even the toughest cops have to earn Bogo's respect—being top of the class at Police Academy just won't cut it!

Four gold stars on collar show high rank.

Not impressed

Chief Bogo is not pleased with having a rabbit police officer. He is convinced that Judy does not belong at the ZPD, and he refuses to give her any detective cases at first, despite her pleas.

Uniform always neatly pressed

Strong, muscled arms

FACT FILE

⭐ **NOTABLE FEATURES:** Thick neck, razor-sharp horns

⭐ **DISLIKES:** Disobedience, time-wasters

⭐ **MOST LIKELY TO:** Fire new recruits without much warning

Straight to the point

Bogo has no time for chitchat in the bullpen. He may be willing to acknowledge birthdays, but he won't waste his time introducing new recruits.

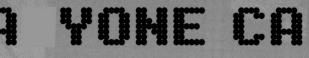

JH0178

JH03056

JH0257

JH011

JH3

ABOUT ME   NEWS   COOL THINGS

My first day at work

I was incredibly excited to start my new job at the ZPD! However, the first day didn't quite go how I had expected it to. Here is what happened...

Morning meeting

It was true that all the ZPD officers were pretty big, but I figured it was part of my job to adjust to change. In this case, I found I could adjust to change by simply standing on my extra-plus-sized rhinoceros chair.

First assignment

So, it turned out that my first assignment wasn't exactly what I thought it would be—I got put on parking duty. I tried to tell Chief Bogo that I could take on a missing mammal case (I was the best student in the academy, thank you very much), but—well, he was a bit bull-headed.

FAMILY   CONTACT

Parking duty

My goal was 100 tickets for the day, but I upped that to 200, before noon! I made it, too, plus another ticket I gave myself. 201!

Up to no good

I hate to admit it, but I got conned by a fox today! He lied to me, he carried out a scam—and he even called me a "dumb bunny!" I decided that fox had better watch his back, because I was going to keep an eye out for him. And wet cement.

Dinner for one

After a tough day, I had a microwave meal of one single carrot for dinner. I could hear my noisy neighbors, Kudu and Oryx Pootosser, shouting all night long. I really hoped the next day would be better...

8 LIKES – 1 COMMENT – SHARE THIS

BONNIE HOPPS: We love you, honey! Parking duty is a fine job! xxx

JUDY'S OFFICER KIT

Judy has always longed to put on the ZPD uniform! The tough blue suit identifies her as a guardian of law and order. She also has a range of equipment to use when on parking duty.

Trusty notepad

Judy's notepad is good for writing all sorts of information. She likes to jot down lots of descriptions and data—from names and license plates to identifying claw marks.

Meter maid cart

Who needs a flashy new police cruiser vehicle when you can drive a flashing meter cart that tops out at 2mph (3.2kph)?

Ticket dispenser

As soon as Judy's super-sharp bunny ears pick up the "ding" of an expired meter, she types in the car's licence, and her machine spits out a ticket with the fine. Judy loves it! (Owners of the cars do not.)

TRUE OR FALSE?

Judy hands out Junior Officer badge stickers to encourage children to follow their dreams.

Answer: True!

Safety first!

Judy's fluorescent orange vest is not a fashion statement, but it does keep her safe: Drivers always see her. Her smart blue meter maid hat completes the look.

"Officer Hopps. You ready to make the world a better place?"

Judy to her new ZPD coworkers

Official police ID

Breathable fabric suitable for all habitats

Strong body armor

Carrot pen

Judy's chunky carrot pen doesn't just look cool. It contains a voice recorder— and that may come in handy for detective work!

Custom uniform

Judy is the smallest member of the force, so she wears a specially adapted uniform with lighter armor than the rhino cops wear. She also carries lighter-weight gadgets on her utility belt.

Extra tiny kneepads protect from scrapes.

Paw and heel protectors

25

NICK WILDE

Street-smart fox Nick earns a living as a hustler. He's very good at convincing innocent mammals that they need to buy his goods. A fast talker with a quick wit, this crook gave up his dreams of a respectable life long ago. He has no plans to change the world or himself any time soon!

Shady scheme

One of Nick's scams is selling "pawpsicles." His partner, Finnick, makes little paw prints in the snow. Nick then pours melted Jumbo-pop juice into the molds. It freezes into many small pawpsicles.

Bushy tail streams behind as he runs.

TOP 3...
SECRETS

1. Secretly wants to be seen as more than a sly fox.

2. Wanted to be a Zootopia Junior Ranger when young.

3. Bullied by mean prey kids as a cub.

Experienced swindler

Nick's sunglasses have many uses. Sometimes he wears them to look smart or avoid being recognized. Here, they protect his eyes from bright sunshine as he melts down a large Jumbo–pop for his new scheme.

"It's called a hustle, sweetheart." Nick

Relaxed, half-open eyes

Strong stereotypes

Nick knows the stereotypes—bunnies are dumb, sloths are slow, elephants have good memories, and, of course, foxes are sly. He goes along with them whenever it suits his plans!

Loosely-knotted stripy tie

Baggy green shirt has scruffy charm.

FACT FILE

⭐ **LAST KNOWN RESIDENCE:** 1955 Cypress Grove Lane, Zootopia

⭐ **SKILLS:** Quick thinker, likeable, deceptive

⭐ **LIKES:** Gullible animals, dreaming up new hustles

Working together

As soon as he meets Judy, Nick is sure that she's easy to trick. When he is pulled into Judy's detective work, however, he learns that he misjudged her, and himself! He makes a pretty good cop—and a pretty good friend.

FINNICK

Finnick is a teeny-tiny, sweet-looking fennec fox—who also happens to be a talented con artist. Looking like an adorable cub is the perfect way to run all sorts of money-making scams with his partner, Nick. It's okay to be small, so long as the payoff is big!

Large, furry ears listen for sirens.

"You kiss me tomorrow, I'll bite your face off."
Finnick to Nick

Wide eyes look for scam opportunities.

Sucks pacifier as part of disguise.

Master of disguise
Finnick never gets caught by the police. Years of wearing cute baby mammal costumes (the elephant outfit works every time) have made him an expert in seeming innocent.

Baggy elephant romper suit

Deep growl

Finnick may look like a toddler, but he doesn't sound like one! His deep voice is super low, so Nick must do the talking, while Finnick relies on making baby noises—or just trying not to laugh inside his stroller.

Partners in crime

Finnick and Nick work together, often pretending to be father and son. They make a good team, but Nick's jokes about Finnick's diapers and size get old pretty fast.

FACT FILE

⭐ **PERSONALITY:**
Ambitious, irritable

⭐ **LIKES:** Making a quick buck, French rap stars

⭐ **MOST RECENT PAYOFF:**
A wad of cash for a pawpsicle scheme.

Van driver

Finnick loves to drive his van while blasting French rap music. But getting behind the wheel can be tricky, as he sometimes gets pulled over for underage driving.

NICK'S TIPS
FOR A GOOD HUSTLE

Everyone expects a fox to be sly, and to hustle other mammals. But the way that Nick sees it, there's nothing wrong—or illegal—in being smarter than your customers. A fox has got to earn a living somehow, right?

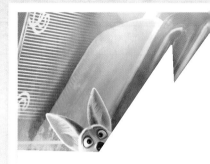

1. IDENTIFY YOUR PRODUCT
Get something that everyone loves. Ice cream is always a good choice.

2. PICK YOUR LOCATION
If you want to buy low and sell high, then go to an elephant-sized shop. Jumbeaux's Cafe has gigantic portions.

4. MAKE THE MOST OF WHAT YOU'VE GOT
Once you've bought the goods, divide them into smaller parts and start selling. Melting a Jumbo-pop into dozens of tiny pops is a great scheme!

3. USE A CUTE ACCOMPLICE
Find a tiny fennec fox to dress up as your son who really, really wants to be an elephant when he grows up.

TRUE OR FALSE?

Judy arrests Nick for selling food without a permit.

False! He does have a permit. This fox is always prepared!

6. WASTE NOT

Recycling is a sign of good citizenship. Besides, someone's trash could be someone else's treasure—and that's good for a hustle.

5. TARGET YOUR CUSTOMERS

Lemmings. This is all you need to know: One buys, and the others follow.

7. SELL EVERYTHING

About that treasure? The mice builders in Little Rodentia will pay for red wood. Who said a used pawpsicle stick was worthless?

8. BE PREPARED

Always have your paperwork ready to show to the police. Going to jail is a waste of time.

Officer Hopps is in pursuit! During her second dull day on parking duty, there's a cry for help from a frantic pig. His shop has just been robbed by a weasel! This is Judy's first chance to be a "real" cop.

1. Tight squeeze

The weasel takes off through Little Rodentia. Most ZPD cops cannot fit through the entrance, but Judy can. No time to wait for backup—Judy is determined to catch the thief.

Thieving Weaselton

The thief is none other than Duke Weaselton. His bag is full of stolen Class C Botanical flower bulbs, named *Midnicampum Holicithias*. (Phew! That's not easy to say.)

TRUE OR FALSE?

Chief Bogo thinks that Judy did a great job in catching the weasel thief.

False! He is furious she abandoned her post and caused chaos.

WEASEL!

2. Building support

Judy may not look strong, but she has trained hard to be a cop. When the perp knocks some mouse apartment buildings off balance in her path, Judy uses her powerful hind legs to right the wrong.

3. Step with care

Even a rabbit cop has to be careful where she steps in Little Rodentia. Its tiny inhabitants aren't used to such large mammals barreling through their streets!

4. Perfect catch

Watch out! The thief kicks a giant ornamental donut sign at Judy. It bounces down the street and nearly lands on a little shrew named Fru Fru, but Judy catches it just in time.

5. Pop the weasel!

Judy catches her suspect by collaring him with the huge donut. She proudly rolls him to the ZPD central station— this is her first arrest!

CASE FILE

Emmitt Otterton has disappeared —possibly from his florist shop, possibly from his home, or possibly from somewhere else. Leads: none. Witnesses: none. Resources: none. Basically, there's no way for me, Officer Judy Hopps, to track this missing otter. Or is there...?

Mammal reported missing by: Mrs. Otterton

- Wife of Otterton
- Anxious behaviour
- Described as "super slippery" by Officer Clawhauser.
- Says she is sure something is wrong
- States the disappearance is very out of character for husband.
- Claims that Otterton would never leave their "two beautiful children."

Missing mammal

- Name: Emmitt Otterton
- Current period of unexplained absence: 10 days
- Occupation: florist
- Species: otter

Distinguishing features:

- Straight frame glasses
- Long, thin whiskers
- Brown eyes
- Neatly tied tie
- Green shirt and sweater vest
- Long, powerful tail

If I don't find the mammal in TWO days, Chief Bogo will take my ZPD badge away!

MISSING MAMMAL CASES

Note to file: The ZPD have a total of 14 missing mammal cases across Zootopia (and I wonder if they are all this challenging!)

Last known sighting

- Photo shows Otterton walking in the street and eating some sort of treat.
  His shadow implies that it was either early morning or late afternoon.

Evidence: pawpsicle

- Treat identified as a red "pawpsicle."
- Looks an awful lot like the handiwork of a certain fox. Possible link?
- Confirmed: Nick Wilde sold the pawpsicle to Otterton.

Link: Nick Wilde

- Species: fox
- Smirk—suspicious?
- May possess crucial intel needed to track down Otterton.
- How can I make him cooperate?

Wilde recorded (on my carrot pen) boasting about his earnings:

$200 a day, for 20 years = $1,460,000. Amount reported on tax forms: $0.

Penalty for lying on forms: five years in jail. Wilde has agreed to assist my investigation!

NEW LOCATION LEAD

- Wilde is unaware of Otterton's current whereabouts, but claims to know Otterton's last location.

- Next stop: Mystic Spring Oasis! A spa located in Sahara Square.

ASSISTANT MAYOR BELLWETHER

Dawn Bellwether is a gentle, quiet sheep who believes that it is super important for the "little guys" to stick together. She is Zootopia's Assistant Mayor, which means lots of filing and trying to keep track of the mayor's busy diary.

Wool piled high to make her seem a few inches taller.

Large frames magnify innocent-looking eyes.

Smart but practical jacket and dress

Jewelry (nothing flashy, of course)

Little guys together

Bellwether is delighted when Judy takes on a new investigation. Bellwether sees Judy as a fellow "little guy," and just knows Judy will get the job done.

Bright white wool

Assistant Mayor Bellwether's tiny headquarters are actually an old janitor's closet! She claims the bleach fumes in the office help to keep her wool super white.

Keeping a watchful eye

Bellwether makes her desk look homey with a sheep calendar and flowery stickers. She says she is just a "glorified secretary," but her nifty computer holds important data about the entire city. That's a lot of power at her hooftips!

ZOOTOPIA TRAFFIC NETWORK
REGIONAL CAMERA DATA SHARING

Search Address
District of Interest
RAINFOREST
Refine Search Area
CANOPY 12

Crime Region
- Tundra Town
- Rainforest District
- Sahara Square
- Savanna Central
- Downtown
- Little Rodentia

Pushed aside

Bellwether has to snuggle in close to be included in photos with the mayor and new police recruits. Lionheart barely seems to notice her.

FACT FILE

⭐ **LIKES:** Knick-knacks, being appreciated

⭐ **FAVORITE GIFT:** Mug from the mayor saying "World's Greatest Assistant Mayor"

⭐ **DISLIKES:** Predators always being in power

Updating the boss

Bellwether is quick to text the mayor that Judy is taking on the Otterton case. She is eager to tell him that his Mammal Inclusion Initiative is working: A rabbit is doing detective work!

HOW TO BE STREET-SMART

Country bunny Judy has a lot to learn in the big city, but wisecracking Nick knows the streets like the back of his paw. It's important for newcomers and old-timers alike to know the rules of city life.

KEEP CLEAR of squirrels with flashing lights and "Wide Load" signs—they may be towing elephants.

DO NOT HOWL NEAR A WOLF PACK
(UNLESS THEY ARE ENGAGED IN AN ORGANIZED HOWL).

AVOID STEPPING IN WET CEMENT—
IT'S HARD TO WASH OUT OF FUR.

RODENTS BEWARE:
ELEPHANT TOILETS ARE DANGEROUS.
NO SWIMMING!

MOVING VEHICLE CAUTION:
KEEP TRUNKS, EARS, AND TAILS INSIDE AT ALL TIMES!

NEVER WALK IN FRONT OF AN ONCOMING HERD, UNLESS SHIELDED BY A PORCUPINE.

ALWAYS LOOK FOUR WAYS BEFORE CROSSING THE STREET (RIGHT, LEFT, UP, AND DOWN).

LARGER MAMMALS ARE FORBIDDEN TO OBSTRUCT OR RIDE ON TOP OF MICE TRAINS.

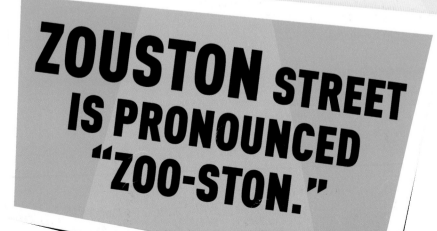

ZOUSTON STREET IS PRONOUNCED "ZOO-STON."

1. Downward dog

2. Half moon

3. Tree pose

Pleasure pool

The spa's pleasure pool is an outdoor haven, surrounded by tropical palm trees and flowers. Animals splash in the clear waters and snooze on warm rocks.

Elephant dozes above waterfall.

bra shakes ter from mane.

MYSTIC SPRING OASIS

This awesome spa is the best place in the city to chill out and feel good. Dudes of all types are seriously welcome here, from business yaks to bear cops. Visitors can relax with meditation, yoga, hot springs, and lots of warm mud. No soap allowed!

Take a break

On entering the spa, all mammals are encouraged to breathe in the goodness of incenses and stinky bodily odors. The rooms are kept dark and quiet to provide a soothing environment.

The naturalist life

Ice-cold drinking fountains help guests cool down after hot volleyball games. The fact that guests exercise in the nude also keeps them cool—the spa is a naturalists' club, which means all the animals are naked!

Ideal rocky spot to bask in sun's heat.

Exotic "bird of paradise" flower

Pink polka dot inner tube

41

YAX

Hippie Yax is the naked yak on Mystic Spring Oasis's front desk. This laid-back dude doesn't seem to notice much going on around him. But to his own surprise, he can tell Judy everything Otterton did during his last visit to the spa, plus the exact time and weather!

Forgetful elephant

Yax takes Judy and Nick to speak to Nanga the elephant, Otterton's yoga instructor. Nanga can't remember anything about the otter. Not all elephants have awesome memories...

A warm welcome

Yax lights lots of candles on the front desk, to create a welcoming atmosphere for newcomers. The glow also helps him examine the photo of Otterton that Judy gives him.

FACT FILE

⭐ **AGE:** It doesn't matter, dude.

⭐ **DISLIKES:** Clothes, deodorant

⭐ **HOBBIES:** Chanting, burning incense

In the zone

Yax won't let guests interrupt his meditation. The more they try to bother him, the louder he chants. At first, he thinks Judy has come to sell Bunny Scout Cookies!

Constant cloud of flies buzz around him.

CRACK
THE CASE
Yax's surprising ability to remember every detail gives Judy and Nick the license plate of the car Otterton got into—29THD03.

Shaggy hair hasn't been washed in a long time!

Mystic orange beads and green charm

Nudity is natural

Judy is shocked to see that Yax—and every other mammal at the spa—is naked. She is even more shocked when Nick takes off his pants, too!

The body is a temple

Yax believes that his body is awesome, and he wants to keep it pure and natural. This means that he never cuts his hair, wears clothes, or uses soap.

Meditating in the lotus pose

DMV OFFICES

The Department of Mammal Vehicles has the big job of keeping records of all the vehicles in Zootopia, from towering giraffe mobiles to tiny mouse cars. Fortunately, the staff are good (if a little slow) at their jobs!

Heavy eyelids

Long lines and red tape

The DMV's workers are very friendly, but they are all sloths—the slowest animals in Zootopia. If you need to renew your license, make sure that you have plenty of time to spare.

DID YOU KNOW?

Even the tiniest rodent vehicles must be registered at the DMV.

A cup of strong coffee

Slowest Employee of the Month

YOU WANT IT WHEN?

NEXT WINDOW →

Slow service

Any mammal about to head into the DMV should enjoy the sunshine while they can. By the time they make it outside again, the day will be over.

Favor from a friend

It's a good thing that know-it-all Nick has a longtime pal who works at the DMV. He can help Judy with her investigation by tracking a license plate.

45

FLASH

Friendly sloth Flash is happy to help anyone who comes to his desk at the DMV—but he won't be quick about it! Nick assures Judy that Flash can track a license plate. What he doesn't mention is just how long it will take.

CRACK THE CASE

Judy and Nick learn that Emmitt Otterton was last seen in a car that is registered to Tundratown Limo-Service.

Sloths type on the tips of their long claws.

Paperwork mountain

Between printing, stapling, and stamping documents, the sloths' paperwork tends to pile up! However, they're never too busy to share a good joke with one other.

Tiresome typist

Judy can't believe how slowly Flash types. One DMV worker was timed typing one letter or number every 10 seconds. That's an average rate of one word per minute!

Say cheese!

Flash's colleague takes ID photos of the customers. It takes such a long time that most mammals struggle to keep smiling for the camera.

Running out of time

Flash doesn't notice Judy is in a rush. He takes so long to look up the plate number (partly due to Nick interrupting his work) that it is dark when they finally leave. They only have 36 hours left to solve the case!

Flash usually has a sleepy smile.

Nick's pal

Flash is a friend of Nick's. At least, that's what Nick says. It's hard to prove, as it would take too long for Flash to confirm or deny the friendship.

It takes Flash an hour to tie his tie.

Flash doesn't move enough to wrinkle his shirt.

"Flash, Flash, hundred yard dash!"
Nick

MR. BIG AND FRU FRU

Mr. Big is the biggest little crime boss in Tundratown. Many mammals are terrified of him—even other criminals! His daughter, Fru Fru, on the other hand is a far sweeter shrew.

Future bride

As an excited bride-to-be, Fru Fru loves nothing more than planning her perfect wedding. This shrew has led a privileged life, but her heart is as big as her hair. She never forgets an act of kindness.

Dramatic beehive hairdo with flowers

Golden hoop earrings

Shopping nightmare

Fru Fru's idea of a great day is shopping with her friends and gossiping about fashion. It certainly doesn't involve nearly being squashed by a giant, falling donut!

Skirt of the finest silk

Wedding dress has beautiful lace sleeves.

Beware the ice

Mr. Big has a quick way to deal with animals who cross him—a big pit of ice, hidden under a trapdoor! Nick and Judy are nearly thrown into it by Mr. Big's bodyguards. Luckily, Fru Fru tells her daddy that Judy saved her life and the pair are spared.

CRACK THE CASE

Mr. Big's limo contains key evidence: Otterton's wallet and strange scratch marks! Judy and Nick must find the chauffeur, Manchas—he may know where Otterton is.

Riches and respect

Mr. Big's criminal activities have made him a wealthy shrew and every crook in Zootopia knows that his high position demands respect. The mini mob boss has an old grudge for Nick, who once swindled him!

Bushy eyebrows good for hiding expression.

Expensive three-piece wedding suit

Extravagant gold and wooden chair

FACT FILE

⭐ **OCCUPATION:** Crime boss

⭐ **DISLIKES:** Mammals that mess with his family

⭐ **LIKES:** Cannoli pastries, Jerry Vole CDs

MR. BIG'S COMPOUND

The city's most powerful crime boss runs his business from a compound in the middle of freezing Tundratown. Polar bear bodyguards patrol its many icy buildings and long corridors.

Icicles form in the chilly air.

No trespassers allowed

Mr. Big's snowy home is gated and guarded. Take a hint: Don't enter the compound unless you're invited. And if you are invited, you may want to leave town fast!

Never forgotten

Mr. Big loved his grandmama, and has created a shrine in her memory. He keeps her picture on a snow-covered shelf, along with flowers and two lit candles. Nothing is too good for grandmama!

Wedding venue

Mr. Big's home is the perfect venue for his daughter's marriage. The shrew guests dine on tiny pieces of wedding cake, and dance among the teeny-weeny party tables and chairs.

Huge bodyguard stands to attention.

Mr. Big's little chair sits on top of the desk

Telephone for important calls

Scary surroundings

Mr. Big's study has a classic look with tall bookshelves and a large, wooden desk. At first, Judy thinks the wealthy owner must be one of the giant polar bears—not a tiny Arctic shrew with a high-pitched voice.

Lavish rug hides a trap door

There are lots of different mammals in Zootopia, which means lots of different personalities! From dreamers and rebels, to leaders and those happy to just follow the herd, find out who you are by taking the quiz below.

Would you like to live in a big, bustling city?

Yes

Do you lose patience quickly?

No

No

You are like Stu Hopps. You prefer a calmer life away from the noise and traffic. You love nature and having your family nearby.

Yes

You are like Chief Bogo. You are a natural leader, and you like to get to the point quickly, without idle chitchat!

Yes

You are like Mr. Big. You may be small, but you wield a lot of power. You know loyalty is the most important quality.

Do you rely on large sidekicks to ice your enemies?

No

Do you believe anyone can be anything?

Yes

You are like Judy Hopps. You have a positive attitude and big dreams. You're not afraid to be different.

No

You are like Nick Wilde. You are realistic and street-smart. But underneath your tough shell lies a friendlier side.

MANCHAS

Big, strong jaguar Manchas lives deep in the steamy Rainforest District. He is also the key witness in Judy's case! His job as Mr. Big's limo driver makes him the last mammal to have seen Emmitt Otterton before he disappeared.

A difficult passenger

Manchas always keeps an eye out for trouble in the rearview mirror. While driving Otterton, a commotion in the backseat is all the warning Manchas gets, before the otter attacks him!

Rainforest home

Nick and Judy follow a tip from Mr. Big to find Manchas's home. The Rainforest District is full of slippery walkways that lead to moss-covered houses, built inside tree trunks.

Careful pawsteps taken across wobbly bridge.

Jaguar gone wild

Manchas is usually a calm, gentle jaguar, but he has barely finished telling Nick and Judy about Otterton going wild when he turns savage, too! The jaguar drops down on all fours and then leaps to attack the pair. It takes quick thinking and teamwork to stop him.

Manchas's home built inside hollow tree trunk.

Lamp glows over Manchas's front door.

Swinging wooden ropebridge stretched high above forest floor.

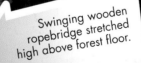

FACT FILE

⭐ **LIVES:** Just off the corner of Vine and Tujunga

⭐ **LIKES:** Wet, rainy climates, comfy clothes, *Cat Fancy* magazine

⭐ **DISLIKES:** Chauffeuring crazy limo passengers

Savage beasts

After Manchas disappears, Nick and Judy track him to Cliffside Asylum. This dark, old hospital also holds the 14 missing mammals that the ZPD have been searching for. All of them have gone savage!

SPLIT IN TWO

Zootopia is in turmoil! Judy's speech stating that all the missing savage animals are predators has accidentally caused chaos. There are protests in the streets and arguments over the airwaves as prey and predators disagree. Some want peace, but others want war...

PREDATORS

Breaking news! Officer Hopps admits predators may be going wild due to their DNA. She stated, "maybe they're reverting back to their savage ways" and hinted that all predators could potentially be dangerous!

TRAVEL TROUBLE

Predators are facing hostile behavior from prey animals on public transportation.

PREY VS. PRED

A celebrity TV show host has insulted his tiger interviewee, saying the attacks were "bound to happen" and accusing his guest of trying to "sweep the pred-prey divide under the rug."

PREY

Marvin 6:44pm
I'm moving my mouse family away from here. Prey aren't safe anymore!

Bob 6:48pm
This is crazy! We've been neighbors for years! You've got nothing to fear from us predators.

Muriel 6:51pm
Hey lion, go back to the swamps!

Bob 6:53pm
I'm from the savannah!

ANOTHER ATTACK!
CHINCHILLA IN HOSPITAL

A chinchilla has been seriously wounded by a savage polar bear in the 27th attack on prey animals to date. No explanation has yet been given for this vicious act.

"NEXT UP on Zoot Radio: we discuss whether predators should be muzzled."

PEACE & UNITY FOR ALL ANIMALS!

JUDY'S WHO'S WHO

My first case is a tough one! It's really important for police officers to make lots of notes to keep track of each lead, witness, and suspect. Hopefully they will help me figure out who took Emmitt Otterton... and why.

Otterton went savage and attacked C, then vanished. C left with black eye and scratches.

A: NICK WILDE

B: MR. BIG

C: MANCHAS

A's pawpsicle goods spotted in the last known sighting photo of Otterton.

B employed Otterton as a florist for his daughter's wedding.

Polar bear fur, Otterton's wallet, and claw marks found in B's limo.

C stated Otterton was yelling about "night howlers." What are they?

B is mad at A for selling him a pricey rug—made with fur from a skunk's butt.

C also went savage and disappeared. Kidnapped by wolves and taken to Cliffside Asylum.

58

CLIFFSIDE ASYLUM

Creepy old hospital. Do the wolves work here? Wolves = night howlers?

F let me access her computer to watch the CCTV traffic videos— this helped me track down C to the asylum.

D: MAYOR LIONHEART

E: DUKE WEASELTON

F: ASSISTANT MAYOR BELLWETHER

D spotted at asylum. What is he doing here? All 14 missing mammals, plus C, found in cages. They've all gone savage!

Why did E steal flower bulbs from that pig's shop?

F has some unusual ideas about prey animals. Are there things that she isn't telling me?

D ordered the mammals to be kidnapped and held captive. He wants to hush everything up. What is going on?

E admitted he was told to drop off the flowers at a deserted subway station. Why?

59

"...the more we try to understand one another, the more exceptional each of us will be..."

Tricky Finnick

"This adorable fox really did look like an innocent kid with his pacifier, but he turned out to be a crook. Later I realized that he does have a heart—he told me how to find Nick when I needed him." —Judy

DID YOU KNOW?

Nick and Judy's first duty as police partners was to patrol the Skunk Pride Parade!

What a team!

"So, we cracked the biggest mystery in Zootopia, and look at us now. I've become a cop, and we're the best partners in the ZPD! I still can't resist the odd dumb bunny joke, but Judy knows I love her." —Nick

Sweet-looking scammer

"Check out this seemingly meek sheep! Her big, wide eyes and white curls make her look all soft and fuzzy, right? Look again, my friend. Look again. This power-hungry criminal mastermind was looking out for herself." —Nick

Dumb bunny

"When I first met her, I thought Judy was just some dumb bunny from the countryside. And okay, she may still live in dreamland sometimes, but she's smarter than she looks... she hustled me!" —Nick

DON'T JUDGE A MAMMAL
BY ITS FUR!

Stereotypes are still a big problem in modern Zootopia. Who sees a sheep without thinking "sweet?" How about elephants who "never forget?" It's taken the unlikely team of a fox and a rabbit to help change the attitudes of an entire city!

Not so confident

"I was pretty surprised to see how scared Nick was of Mr. Big! Seeing his vulnerable side is really something." —Judy

Mr. Big?!

"We were surrounded by huge polar bears— who would have thought the famous mob boss, Mr. Big, was a tiny Arctic shrew? AND he helped us solve the case!" —Judy

OFFICER ENTRANCE EXAM

Write your name here

NICK WILDE

You are about to take the officer entrance exam.
ZPD is proud to support the Mammal Inclusion Initiative:
Whether you are predator or prey, large or small,
we welcome you to the force.

You will have 30 minutes to complete this multiple choice test.

NO HOWLING OR BATHROOM BREAKS ALLOWED.

PLEASE READ EACH QUESTION CAREFULLY AND SELECT THE CORRECT ANSWER.

1   *Scooping ice cream with an ungloved trunk is:*
- a: A Class 3 Health Code Violation.
- b: A good way to sample the goods.
- c: An acceptable practice in ice-cream parlors.

2   *It is legal to transport goods across borough lines without a permit.*
- a: True.
- b: Maybe. It depends on whether you are transporting something that tastes good.
- c: False.

3   *Which of the following is considered an emergency:*
- a: Rubber platypus stuck in a sink drain.
- b: Real platypus stuck in a sink drain.
- c: Traffic jam.

4   *Mammal officers on parking duty should be prepared to:*
- a: Ticket only large vehicles.
- b: Ticket all illegally parked vehicles.
- c: Ignore illegally parked vehicles that are pink.

5   *10-91 is police radio code for:*
- a: Animal dressed in a tutu sighted.
- b: Officer on duty requires a bathroom break.
- c: Savage animal sighted.

6   *It is illegal to enter a property without a warrant.*
- a: True.
- b: False.
- c: True, unless the officer has a good reason, such as spotting a suspicious figure climbing over the fence.

Answers:
1. a   2. c   3. b   4. b   5. c   6. c

ACKNOWLEDGMENTS

Editor Ruth Amos
Senior Designer Lynne Moulding
Editorial Assistant Lauren Nesworthy
Additional design David McDonald, Toby Truphet
Pre-Production Producer Marc Staples
Senior Producer Lloyd Robertson
Managing Editor Sadie Smith
Managing Art Editor Ron Stobbart
Art Director Lisa Lanzarini
Publisher Julie Ferris
Publishing Director Simon Beecroft

First American Edition, 2016
Published in the United States by DK Publishing
345 Hudson Street, New York, New York 10014

Page design copyright © 2016 Dorling Kindersley Limited
DK, a Division of Penguin Random House LLC
16 17 18 19 10 9 8 7 6 5 4 3 2 1
002–280402–Jan/2016

A catalog record for this book is available
from the Library of Congress.

ISBN 978-1-4654-4428-8

DK books are available at special discounts
when purchased in bulk for sales promotions,
premiums, fund-raising, or educational use.
For details, contact: DK Publishing Special Markets,
345 Hudson Street, New York, New York 10014
SpecialSales@dk.com

Printed and bound in the USA

A WORLD OF IDEAS:
SEE ALL THERE IS TO KNOW

www.dk.com
www.disney.com